INSTANT OFFICIANT:

A No-Nonsense Guide to the
Perfect Wedding Ceremony

By Chris Cote

Table of Contents

Introduction

I officiated my first wedding in 2006 at the request of my friends Scott and Lindsey. To put it mildly, I had no idea what I was doing. I scoured the library and the internet for advice on where to start, and I was surprisingly disappointed with what I found. There were lots of books detailing the steps for a denominational ceremony, but not many that effectively covered how to craft a customized ceremony for friends. I needed to get it right, as I don't think I had ever been more nervous. After weeks of continuous research and preparation, I eventually managed to cobble together a ceremony that I was proud of.

Despite some minor hiccups on the day (including forgetting to ask people to sit down, which resulted in a few awkward minutes with half of the attendees seated and the other half standing), the ceremony was a success. It was at least enough of the success that other friends began asking me to perform their wedding ceremonies. After performing my third wedding ceremony, I finally produced a template to aid in creating meaningful ceremonies and save myself time.

Word eventually got out that I was the wedding officiant guy, and soon I was being approached by friends and friends-of-friends for advice. I would hand them my template, provide some over-the-phone advice, and send them off to prepare their own ceremonies.

I received a lot of positive feedback about the template, including the occasional "you should write a book." I finally decided to act on that advice, and so here we are. I hope that my 15+ years of experience conducting wedding ceremonies, passed down to you in this no-nonsense guide, will help you prepare for the wonderful, unique experience of officiating a wedding ceremony.

How to Use this Book

This book is designed to be used as an introduction to how to officiate a wedding, and as a reference point when developing and preparing for a wedding ceremony. It covers everything from becoming an ordained minister to creating and performing the ceremony itself, as well as post-wedding tasks. It's a great reference guide for anyone who wants to officiate a wedding, regardless of experience level. It provides plenty of tips and advice on how to make your wedding ceremony unique and memorable. If you're looking to officiate a wedding with style and grace, then this is the book for you!

If you're new to officiating weddings, then you should read the book all the way through before meeting with the couple. You can revisit each section later as a reference guide.

If you're a seasoned pro, then you can skip the chapter about how to become ordained.

If you simply want an example ceremony to

reference, then jump to the last few chapters where I provide full sample ceremonies.

I have attempted to make this book gender-neutral by referring to the "couple" instead of the "bride and groom" when possible. But you will still notice several instances in this book where I use gender pronouns and the terms bride and groom (primarily when discussing traditional order or physical placement during the ceremony). I did this simply for an easier reading experience, and not as a commentary on marriage. When preparing your own ceremony, please swap out the genders and terminology, as appropriate.

Thank you for reading, and I hope you find this book helpful, informative, and inspirational! You'll be on your way to the perfect wedding ceremony in no time.

Who is the Wedding Officiant and What Do They Do?

At its core, a wedding officiant has two jobs: (1) presiding over the ceremony and (2) signing the marriage certificate. They are an important part of any wedding because without them the wedding couldn't happen.

Officiants are also sometimes asked to take on additional responsibilities, including mailing the marriage certificate, holding the rings, queuing the DJ, or frankly anything else the couple requests. I've even been asked to stash liquor for the groomsmen.

But in reality, the officiant plays a much larger role. They set the tone for the occasion, and for better or worse, their words and actions may be remembered by the attendees for years to come.

I recall attending a friend's wedding where the officiant got the groom's name wrong. Not once, but twice, including when he was asked to kiss the bride. The attendees stared at each other in disbelief. It was bad.

I'm not telling you this to scare you. Officiating a wedding is not actually that hard. You just need to understand that your role is important. With the right knowledge and preparation, you can make the couple's wedding day memorable... in a good way.

Now that you understand the role of an officiant, let's take a look at how to become one.

Get Ordained: How to Become a Wedding Officiant

One of the most common misconceptions about being a wedding officiant is that it's only available to religious people and priests. Good news: you don't need to dump your significant other and join the priesthood to perform a wedding ceremony. You also don't need to attend rabbinical school. But what you do need to do is become an ordained minister. Thankfully, we live in the modern era, so that can be accomplished with just a few clicks over the internet.

Another misconception about being a wedding officiant is that only religious people can do it, but that's not the case. When choosing a Ministry, there are a lot of different ordination options out there. Some are religious (e.g., World Christianship Ministries), some are spiritual (e.g., Universal Life Church), and some are completely non-religious (e.g., the American Marriage Ministries). Joining a ministry varies in cost from free to several hundred dollars. Ultimately, it depends on your budget, religious preferences, and whether the couple has a preference.

Before exploring your different options, however, you need to understand that each US state has its own requirements for wedding officiants, and there may also be local laws that apply. Some states will recognize any online Ministry, some online recognize certain Ministries, some don't recognize online ordination but do permit mail-order ordination, and others require you to be registered with the local government. For guidance on what different jurisdictions require, and how to get ordained, you can check out instantofficiant.com/resources.

With this in mind, you must ask the couple about where the wedding will take place, so you can validate that you are permitted to perform the wedding ceremony. Sometimes you might need to take additional steps to officiate. I am personally an ordained minister with several different organizations because my previous ordinations weren't permitted in certain jurisdictions.

What happens if you can't meet the ordination requirements of the state, but the couple still wants you to officiate? Fear not, you may have another option. One common approach in this scenario is for the couple to get married in a courthouse, and for you to perform the ceremony as if it never happened. The main difference here is that you would not be signing a marriage certificate (because that's already been handled), and you may need to keep quiet about the courthouse wedding if the family doesn't know about it.

Sections of the Ceremony

It may come as a surprise, but there is no standard composition of a wedding ceremony. How you compose any individual ceremony will vary.

Below is a list of common sections of a wedding ceremony. Note that terminology used to describe the various sections may vary by source. I explore each of these wedding ceremony sections in greater detail in their own chapters later in the book. If you're not at least somewhat familiar with these different wedding ceremony sections, then I recommend you read ahead before having your initial consultation with the couple.

1. Prelude/ Seating of the Guests
2. Processional
3. Giving of the Bride
4. Words of Welcome/ Introduction
5. Special Dedication/ Remembrances
6. Address to Congregation/ Opening Remarks
7. Readings
8. Support of Community

9. Declaration of Intent/ Charge
10. Objection
11. Exchange of Vows
12. Exchange of Rings
13. Unity Ceremony
14. Words of Encouragement/ Final Blessing
15. Pronouncement of Marriage
16. The Kiss
17. Presentation
18. Recessional

Boy, that's an awfully long list. The reason it's so long is that (a) many of these sections are very short and (b) most of these sections are completely optional. In fact, the only required portions of the wedding ceremony are the "Declaration of Intent" and "Pronouncement of Marriage". Everything else is optional (but many are traditional).

Also, to give you a sense of what a full ceremony may look like (and to satisfy those that want the done-for-you treatment), I've included a few full ceremonies in the "Sample Ceremony Script" chapters of this book.

The Couples Questionnaire

After officiating several weddings, I designed and implemented a practice that has proven to be invaluable: the couples questionnaire. This is a questionnaire that I send out to all of the couples who want me to officiate their wedding, regardless of how well I know them. This questionnaire helps me get to know the couple better so that I can write an original, personal ceremony with an authentic voice. If you haven't done this before, I encourage you to implement it.

Have each person fill out the couples questionnaire before you meet with them. Ask them to complete the questionnaires individually, and not to share them with each other. Their responses may give you amazing insight into their story and wishes for the future that you can use to guide your ceremony script.

My questionnaire covers topics such as how they met, their first date, their favorite memories as a couple, and funny stories about their courtship that they wouldn't mind sharing.

You can visit instantofficiant.com/resources for the current version of my couples questionnaire. Please feel free to modify it to suit your needs, and let me know if you have additions that I should consider implementing. You can contact me at contact@instantofficiant.com.

Once you've reviewed the questionnaires, you're ready to meet with the couple to discuss the ceremony.

The First Meeting with the Couple

The best way to ensure that the ceremony is perfect for the couple is to get a sense of their style, expectations, and preferences. Before you start preparing the wedding ceremony, it's always best to have an initial meeting to flesh this out. This meeting should generally take less than 30-minutes and can be done in-person, on the phone, or over a video call. The earlier you can have this discussion in the process, the better, because it leaves you more time to prepare.

Below are some of the topics that you want to discuss during that first meeting.

Topic 1: Dates/ Location/ Time Commitment

When and where are the wedding and rehearsal taking place? How long are you expected to be at the rehearsal and wedding? Do they expect you to attend for an hour before the ceremony? Are they expecting you to hang around after the reception until late in the evening? Which events you're invited to and for how long will depend on how well you know the couple, and their personal preference. You just need to make sure that you are in the right place at the right time.

Topic 2: Attire

What should you wear to the wedding? You don't want to wear something too casual or too formal. If you are unsure, it's always best to ask the couple. Many officiants choose to dress in a black suit with a white shirt and black tie, a black pantsuit with a white shirt, or a black dress. Always ask permission before wearing something flashier. Keep in mind that you will be in at least some of the wedding pictures, so choose something that makes you feel comfortable in the images.

Topic 3: Length of Ceremony

How long do they want the ceremony to last? Most couples prefer ceremonies that are around 20-25 minutes long, but they can vary widely. I've witnessed a wedding ceremony that was 20 seconds long and performed in a Washington, DC crosswalk during a light change. My personal speed run was 7 minutes (hi, Eric & Elaine). You should have seen the look on the groom's uncle's face when he tried to sneak in late only to realize the couple was already exiting.

Topic 4: Content of the Ceremony

This is probably the most important topic that you will discuss with the couple. Is there a theme they want you to use? What sections of the ceremony does the couple want to include? Be prepared to offer recommendations, and let them know that you may follow up with additional recommendations later if you're not hitting their preferred length.

Topic 5: Religion

Does the couple want you to mention God or not? Wedding ceremonies can be personalized and non-religious - they don't have to contain references to God or any other deity. If they do want you to mention God, are they looking for a specific denomination or just a general reference? Do they have any specific requests about readings or prayers? If the couple does not want you to mention God, what kind of wording can you use in place of a religious blessing?

Topic 6: Topics to Avoid

You should always make it a point to ask what topics the couple is not comfortable with you discussing in their ceremony. Maybe they've been living together for several years but the family doesn't know? Maybe one of them comes from a family that is very conservative and the other person's family has a tendency to speak their mind? Make sure you know what you can and can't discuss in the wedding ceremony.

Topic 7: Other Interested Parties

Is there a wedding planner that you should be coordinating with? Or is a sibling, friend, or parent helping to organize the wedding? You should know so you can coordinate logistics, which will spare the couple additional stress.

Topic 8: Makeup of the Wedding Party

How many bridesmaids, groomsmen, ushers, etc. will be in the wedding party? You may be asked to coordinate how they walk down the aisle, or who stands where during the ceremony.

After discussing all of these topics, you should have a good understanding of what the couple is looking for in their wedding ceremony. You can now start preparing the actual ceremony.

Writing the Ceremony

With the couples questionnaire in hand, and notes from your meeting, it is now time to start writing the wedding ceremony. But where do you start?

Step 1: Decide on Uniqueness

First, decide if you want to write your own ceremony or copy from somewhere else. This choice may be dictated by timing. If the couple gives you sufficient notice, you may be able to write your own words. If you are short on time, or just want a little help getting started, consider using one of the ceremony scripts we've included in this book or other inspiration.

Even if you plan to write your own words, do not be afraid to borrow parts and pieces from ceremony samples. Many of the sample ceremony snippets featured in this book are common phrasings that I gathered from various websites over the years. If you are looking for snippets beyond those that we include in this book, then a simple Google search should produce plenty of options. You may have better luck with your online searches if you search by section of the ceremony (e.g., "sample wedding vows") rather than searching for full sample ceremonies (although those also exist).

If you are borrowing from other sources, try to find a ceremony that has the same tone of voice as you do, reads well, and reflects the couple's personalities (and tweak it as necessary). It does not matter how you created their wedding masterpiece as long as the components have been woven together intelligently and respect the couple's vision.

Step 2: Find a Theme

Next, identify a common theme that you can pull throughout the script. The theme is the message of your story. This could be something like "love" or "hope." Every time you mention the theme in the ceremony, it should be to reinforce the idea that both partners are feeling these sentiments.

Think about your job as a wedding officiant being to use language that will evoke these feelings in your audience. If you mention "love" or "hope," be sure that you are planting positive thoughts into the heads of your guests, not upsetting them.

Need some inspiration? In addition to "love" or "hope," some other themes to consider are:

- Caring
- Commitment

- Friendship
- Trust
- Respect
- Unity
- Appreciation
- Empowerment
- Exploration
- Growth
- A New Family
- New Beginnings
- Two Hearts become One

Ultimately, the theme you choose will depend on the love story you are telling.

Depending on the couple's preferences, you may want to consult them after picking a theme. Asking for their input before you have written too much can save time and embarrassment if they had another idea in mind.

Step 3: Decide on the Tone

Once you know the story you plan to tell, decide on the atmosphere you want to set when telling it. Some common tones to employ are: joyful, humorous, silly, witty, playful, serene, serious, and philosophical.

If you plan to go with humorous, silly, or witty, make sure the couple agrees with your choice. This isn't open mic night at the local comedy club, and it is up to you to make sure the couple's wishes are respected.

Step 4: Establish the Framework

Create an outline identifying the sections of the ceremony you would like to include, and the order in which you'll include them. Refer back to the "Sections of the Ceremony" chapter and your discussions with the couple. You may need to revisit this framework later if it doesn't align with the couple's preferred ceremony length.

Step 5: Write Section-by-Section

Once you have a framework, it should be easier to start writing. Remember that you can always change your outline later if needed, so don't worry about every sentence being perfect before going ahead and beginning the first draft.

You should write the script in the first person. Writing in the first person helps to make the script sound conversational and will help your audience feel like they know you. To make this work, keep sentences short and use contractions. Also, speak from the heart and write what you would say if it were a conversation with a friend.

You may also want to consider including quotes in your ceremony. There are many famous love quotes out there, or you could choose something more specific to the couple. Just be sure that the quote you choose is short and sweet, and does not take away from your own words.

Finally, consider weaving in stories from the couple. This can be anything from funny stories about how they met to touching anecdotes about their loved ones. The more you can share about who these people are, the better. Revisit the couple's questionnaire that you had them fill out before your first meeting for inspiration.

Step 6: Time It

Before perfecting the script, time it. If the couple has given a ceremony length to shoot for, read it aloud and time yourself to ensure you meet their expectations. Don't rely on page length alone.

If the ceremony length is too long, then you'll need to make cuts. If the ceremony is too short, then you'll need to expand it.

You should start by cutting or adding to the sections that are already in the framework. If you need to add or remove an entire section, make sure to consult the couple first and be prepared to offer recommendations.

Step 7: Review and Revise

Once you've nailed the timing and enjoy your first draft enough that it feels like a real wedding ceremony (and not just words on paper), it's time to review and revise. Print it out and look at it with fresh eyes to find any inconsistencies or unclear points. If you have the luxury of time, then stepping away from your script for a few days before reviewing and revising will help.

Make sure that you are staying on theme, and weaving a cohesive narrative. Tightening up the script is essential at this stage. The best ceremonies are simple yet elegant, and should not sound like a high school graduation speech.

Don't forget about transitional sentences and phrases that link one section to another. You will want to keep these because they help piece together the overall story of the ceremony.

Once you feel confident in your ceremony, take what you've written and work with another person to make it better. Consider showing or reading it to a friend, and pay attention to their feedback.

To help ensure success, try to have a final draft that is ready to be performed at least two weeks before the wedding day.

Step 8: Send for Approval (if needed)

Some couples may ask you to send a copy of the ceremony for edits and approval. In my experience, it's not very common, but don't be offended if the couple asks. After all, it's their big day!

If the couple requested approval, then send it to them for review after you finalize the wording. If they have any changes, then be prepared to make those updates quickly. If the changes are extensive, ask them if they want you to do a final draft and send it for approval again.

That covers the main steps you need to follow to write a wedding ceremony. In the next several chapters, we will dive into the different sections of a wedding ceremony, and what you can expect.

The Ceremony: Prelude/ Seating of the Guests

The prelude occurs before the ceremony, and it's when everyone who isn't in the processional should take their seats so the ceremony may begin. If there are ushers, then they will escort people to their seats. If there are no ushers, then people will seat themselves.

Traditionally, there's a bride's side and a groom's side of the aisle. The bride's side is on the left when you're facing towards the altar, and the groom's side is on the right when you're facing towards the altar.

The prelude usually begins about 30 minutes before the start of the ceremony, depending on how large the wedding is. No one wants to be that guy that walks in during the ceremony!

This is a good time for you to make sure that you have everything you need, including your script, the rings (which are usually with the best man if there is one), and anything else that is going to be involved in the ceremony such as unity candles.

Otherwise, just sit back, relax, and get ready for the show to start.

The Ceremony: Processional

The processional is the official start of the ceremony and is when the wedding party and immediate family walk down the aisle and take their places. Before the processional can begin, the guests should be seated. Usually, there's a music cue, and people understand that they need to take their seats, but sometimes you need to make an announcement. Ask the couple in advance if they'd like you to make an announcement for everyone to take their seats, or if the DJ (if there is one) will be making an announcement.

Different sources and traditions dictate different orders for the processional. If the couple is working with a wedding planner, then they may already know exactly what order they want to proceed in. If not, then they'll likely lean on you for recommendations. I'll give you my thoughts on best practices, but also provide some other perspectives so the couple can make an informed decision.

This is the order and structure that I recommend. It's

not entirely traditional, but it's easy to follow and helpful for spacing because you don't need to save room in the lineup at the altar for people who are entering later. Members of the wedding party should be on either the bride's side or groom's side when entering, so they don't need to switch sides after they arrive at the altar.

1. The officiant - The officiant should be standing at the altar when the processional begins. I usually enter from the side, but it's also acceptable to walk down the aisle if the couple requests it, or if the venue doesn't have a convenient side entrance.

2. The groom with his mother - I find that the mothers often enjoy walking down the aisle with their sons.

3. The best man and maid of honor

4. The groomsmen and bridesmaids - Enter in the order that they are going to be lined up behind the best man and maid of honor at the altar. If there's not an even number of groomsmen and bridesmaids, then someone will walk alone.

5. The ushers in pairs (optional) - Sometimes the ushers are officially part of the wedding party and walk down the aisle, but in most cases, they will already have taken their seats before the processional begins. Ask the couple their preference. Either way, it's unlikely that they will be standing at the altar during the ceremony, and should take their seats somewhere in the first few

rows.

6. The ring bearer (if there is one) - Because this role is usually filled by a young man, they often don't stand at the altar throughout the wedding ceremony. Instead, they'll walk down the aisle and then sit with a waiting parent in the first few rows.

7. The flower girl (if there is one) - Like the ring bearer, the flower girl will often walk down the aisle and then sit with a waiting parent in the first few rows.

8. The bride with her father - This is a big moment, so there's usually a music queue and people should stand for the entrance. You should plan to cue the DJ or the band and tell everyone to stand before the bride proceeds down the aisle (if the guests don't do so automatically).

Note that there are some common modifications to the order above, and these modifications can be combined together to form a unique order for the processional.

- **Modification 1**: Have the groom and the best man enter from a side door after the officiant enters, and wait at the altar during the processional.

- **Modification 2**: The maid of honor and best man walk together immediately before the bride (after the groomsmen and bridesmaids). If you do this, then you need to make sure that the wedding party leaves room for the maid of honor and best man to be beside the couple at the altar.

- **Modification 3**: The maid of honor walks alone after the bridesmaids. Again, if you do this, then you need to make sure that the wedding party leaves room for the maid of honor to be beside the bride at the altar.
- **Modification 4**: The ring bearer and flower girl walk together.

Also, be aware that Jewish and Catholic wedding ceremonies have their own specific traditions, which are not covered here (but can be easily found online).

The Ceremony: Giving of the Bride

The giving of the bride is when the officiant asks who is giving away the bride (typically the father-of-the-bride). It occurs immediately after the bride and the father-of-the-bride walk down the aisle, and before the father-of-the-bride takes his seat.

Some couples prefer to omit this portion of the wedding because it suggests that the woman needs permission from her father to get married. Other couples prefer to include it. You should ask the couple their preference in advance.

If you are including this portion of the ceremony, it involves a quick call and response with the father-of-the-bride. You will ask "Who gives this woman to be wedded to this man?" or some variation, and the father-of-the-bride will respond "I do." The groom and the father-of-the-bride will then shake hands, and the father-of-the-bride will take his seat in the first row. You may need to instruct the father-of-the-bride to take a seat, and instruct the groom to come stand next to the bride.

Some common phrasings for this section of the ceremony include:

Example A: *"Who gives this woman to be wedded to this man?"*

Example B: *"Who supports this couple in their marriage?"*

Example C: *"Who supports this woman in her marriage to this man?"*

The Ceremony: Words of Welcome/ Introduction

The words of welcome or introduction are when the officiant welcomes everyone to the ceremony and explains why we are all here. It's traditionally kicked off with "dearly beloved, we are gathered here today…", but you do not need to use those words.

Before you launch into the words of welcome, ask everyone to please take their seats, because they are likely still standing from when the bride walked down the aisle. If you recall from the book's introduction, I learned this lesson the hard way when, during the first wedding ceremony I conducted, I forgot to do this. Some people sat, and some people stood awkwardly until the father-of-the-bride successfully got my attention and reminded me to give the cue to sit. We all had a good laugh about it, but please, learn from my mistakes.

When crafting the words of welcome, you will want to keep it short and sweet. The main concepts that you want to address are (a) explaining why we are all here and

(b) thanking the guests for attending. You can also share a few thoughts on marriage and love, but keep it brief. You'll have an opportunity to speak more in later portions of the ceremony.

Below are some examples for you to consider:

Example A: *"Dearly beloved [or "ladies and gentlemen" or "friends and family"], we are gathered here today to join [GROOM] and [BRIDE] in matrimony [or "holy matrimony" or "to celebrate the wedding of [GROOM] and [BRIDE]"]. You have previously shared and contributed to their lives, and by witnessing their wedding ceremony today, [GROOM] and [BRIDE] invite you to share in their future with them."*

Example B: *"Welcome friends, relatives, and distinguished guests. We're glad you could join us in celebrating love. Our large and ever-changing planet is controlled by love. It is that which makes our human existence meaningful and beautiful. The greatest gift bestowed on humanity is the gift of love freely given between two people."*

The Ceremony: Special Dedication/ Remembrances

The special dedication or remembrances section is when you take time to acknowledge and honor people that can't be there with you (such as deceased relatives or people who are unable to travel), people that have been especially supportive (such as close family members), or people that have traveled great distances to be there in person.

This is not a traditional section of a wedding, and you won't find it in most ceremony guides. But I personally find it to be one of the most impactful and meaningful portions of the wedding. Whether you include this should always be up to the couple, and you should solicit their opinion regarding whether there's anyone that they want to acknowledge. Regardless of the outcome, the couple will be glad that you asked.

Consider the following examples:

Example A – Acknowledging People Who Travelled

Far: *"I would especially like to thank those of you that have traveled far to be here today. We are all glad that you could make it."*

Example B – Acknowledging People that are Joining the Wedding Ceremony Virtually: "I would like to take a moment to recognize two very special guests that are joining us virtually: [NAME] and [NAME]. We wish you could be here in person, but we are so happy that you can witness the wedding on the livestream."

Example C – Acknowledging Family: *"It is my honor to celebrate the family members of [BRIDE] and [GROOM]. Your love, dedication, and fidelity has profoundly shaped their lives. Thank you for showing them the possibilities inherent when loving another."*

Example D – An alternative way of Acknowledging Family: *"It is my honor to thank the family of [BRIDE] and [GROOM] for their unconditional love and dedication. We thank you for being a daily inspiration that shows the satisfaction gained from loving another."*

Example E – Honoring the Deceased: *"At this time, we also honor those people who are not able to be with us in person today, particularly [NAME] and [NAME], who have passed. They are here today in our hearts."*

The Ceremony: Address to Congregation/ Opening Remarks

The address to the congregation (sometimes called the opening remarks) is when you get to speak freely. This portion of the ceremony generally sets the tone of the wedding and is where it's most important to have a coherent theme. This is the officiant's time to shine.

Good topics to focus on are the couple, the definition of marriage, or a combination of both. This is where it is most appropriate to insert anecdotes about the couple, and how they found each other.

If you are feeling stuck, don't worry! The sample ceremony scripts give examples of how to weave in personal stories, and below are some examples that you can use as a starting point when talking about the institution of marriage:

Example A: "In marriage, two people turn to each other in search of a greater fulfillment than either can achieve alone. Marriage is a bold step, taken together, into an unknown future. It is risking who we are for the sake of who we can be. Only in giving of ourselves fully, and sharing our lives with another, can the mysterious process of growth take place. Only in loyalty and devotion bestowed upon another can that which is eternal in life emerge and be known. Two among us, who have stood apart, come together now, to declare their love and to be united in marriage.

The words we say today have no magic or prophetic powers. The power of the wedding vows is merely a reflection of a reality that already exists in the hearts and minds of these two people. [GROOM] and [BRIDE], nothing I can say, or nothing you can say to each other, will ensure a long and happy, satisfying, and committed marriage. Only your love for one another, and your integrity to make your commitment real, can do that."

Example B*: "To borrow from poet Edmund O'Neill, marriage is a promise, made in the hearts of two people who love each other, which takes a lifetime to fulfill. Within the circle of its love, marriage encompasses all of life's most important relationships. A wife and a husband are each other's lover, teacher, listener, critic, and best friend.*

It is into this state that [GROOM] and [BRIDE] wish to enter."

Example C*: "Here are some wonderful words*

[borrowed from 1 Corinthians] that define the true meaning of love:

"Love is patient and kind; Love is not jealous or boastful;

Love is not arrogant or rude; Love does not insist on its own way;

Love does not rejoice at wrong, but rejoices with the right.

Love bears all things, believes all things, hopes all things, endures all things.

Love never fails."

Learning to love each other and to live together in harmony is one of the greatest challenges of marriage. Marriage is not to be entered into lightly, and we are to hold it in high honor at all times."

Example D: *"Love is the reason we are here. In marriage, we not only say, "I love you today", but also, "I promise to love you for all of our tomorrows."*

[GROOM] and [BRIDE], in the days ahead of you, there will be stormy times and good times, times of conflict and times of joy. I ask you to remember this advice:

Never go to bed angry.

Let your love be stronger than your anger.

Learn the wisdom of compromise, for it is better to bend than to break.

Believe the best of your beloved rather than the worst.

Confide in your partner and ask for help when you need it.

Remember that true friendship is the basis for any lasting relationship.

Give your spouse the same courtesies and kindnesses you bestow on your friends.

Say "I love you" every day."

The Ceremony: Readings

R eadings are when one or two friends or family members come to the altar and read a poem, passage, or prayer. Readings are a good way to add a few extra minutes to the ceremony if it is running short, and are a nice way to involve other important people who are not part of the wedding party. I recommend placing the readings in this part of the ceremony lineup (before the declaration of intent), but they can also come later in the ceremony, or be split up if there are multiple readings.

You will need to introduce the readers during the ceremony. Make sure you introduce yourself to the readers before the ceremony, and learn where they are sitting and how to pronounce their names.

It's unlikely that the couple will ask you to select the readings; the couple will either select the readings themselves, or ask the readers to pick. But they may ask you for advice on selecting an appropriate reading. When selecting a reading, you want it to fit in with the broader ceremony. It's particularly important to keep in mind the following five things:

1. **Religion**: Is the ceremony religious or secular? A religious passage in an otherwise secular ceremony will feel out of place, and may even be unwelcome.

2. **Tone**: Does the couple want something serious or funny, uplifting or insightful, etc.?

3. **Theme**: Is there a theme that the couple wants to be highlighted in the readings (e.g., love, commitment, caring, family, etc.)?

4. **Length**: You don't want to choose readings that are too long or too short.

5. **Topics or Depictions to Avoid**: The list will be different for each couple, but there are always topics to avoid. One good example is traditional readings that depict wives as submissive to their husbands. Some couples may happily include such readings, while others would shudder at the thought. When couples allow the reader to choose the passage, it's important that the couple also specifies what they DON'T want.

Please visit instantofficiant.com/resources for suggested readings, which you can also share with the couple.

The Ceremony: Support of Community

The support of community portion of a ceremony is when you ask the guests to commit to supporting the couple's marriage. It's an optional opportunity to get the guests involved.

If you are including this portion of the ceremony, it involves a quick call and response with the guests. You will ask *"Will you who are present here today, surround the couple in love, offering them the joys of your friendship, and supporting them in their marriage?"* or some variation, and the guests will respond *"we will."*

Unlike the "Giving of the Bride" call and response, the guests won't know this is coming or what to say. Therefore, you will need to prompt the guests to stand, tell them how to respond, and prompt them to sit afterward.

Below is an example of how you could incorporate a "Support of Community" call and response:

"Two people in love do not live in isolation. Their love is a source of strength with which they may nourish

not only each other but also the world around them. And in turn, we, their community of friends and family, have a responsibility to this couple. By our steadfast care, respect, and love, we can support their marriage and the new family they are creating today.

Will everyone please rise?

I have an important question for all of you, the appropriate response to which is "we will."

Will you who are present here today, surround [BRIDE] and [GROOM] in love, offering them the joys of your friendship, and supporting them in their marriage?"

The guests would then respond "*we will*," which would conclude the "Support of Community" section of the ceremony.

The Ceremony: Declaration of Intent/ Charge

The declaration of intent (sometimes called the "charge") is the "I do" portion of the ceremony. Unlike many of the other portions of the ceremony, the declaration of intent is not optional; it is mandatory. Many states have it written into their laws because it's an indication that the couple is willingly entering into the marriage. However, you still have a lot of flexibility in the language that is used for the declaration of intent.

Most declarations of intent are a simple statement that the couple promises to treat each other well. The couple could write their own, or choose a standard option like the one below:

"Entering into marriage is a decision that requires careful thought and consideration.

[GROOM], do you understand and accept the responsibilities of marriage, and do you promise to always love, honor, and cherish [BRIDE]?"

[GROOM]: "I do."

"[BRIDE], do you understand and accept the responsibilities of marriage, and do you promise to always love, honor, and cherish [GROOM]?"

[BRIDE]: "I do."

The Ceremony: Objection

The objection portion of the ceremony is when you ask if anyone objects to the couple getting married. If you've ever seen a movie involving a wedding, then you've probably seen a highly dramatized version of this play out. It is optional, but I discourage couples from including it.

If you do include it, there are only a few ways that it can play out, and none of them are great.

1. **No one objects**: Yay. You've just managed to create a few seconds of awkward silence, and nothing has been accomplished.

2. **Someone objects as a joke**: People may chuckle at the time, but it's not really that funny. This is something the couple will remember whenever they reminisce about their wedding. It's supposed to be a day filled with good memories for the couple, and someone just spoiled it (and you gave them that opportunity).

3. **Someone seriously objects**: Oh, boy. Why did

that person get an invite? This isn't the time or the place for these types of shenanigans. Good luck managing this scenario and recovering.

In my opinion, the objection portion is tacky and should be avoided. Ultimately, it's up to the couple, but I encourage you to either (a) not present it as an option or (b) present it as an option but discourage it.

If you are going to include an objection, then consider the following common phrasing:

"If any person can show just cause why they may not be joined together - let them speak now or forever hold their peace."

The Ceremony: Exchange of Vows

The exchange of vows is when the couple makes promises to each other about how they will act as partners in marriage.

The couple can choose to either write their own vows or use generic vows. Some couples want to write their own vows because they feel they are more personal and meaningful. Other couples prefer to use generic vows because it's less pressure on the couple during their wedding day. Either way is acceptable; just ask them their preference.

As the officiant, you will want to cue that it's time to exchange the vows. Below is an example of what you could say:

"We've come to the point of your ceremony where you're going to say your vows to one another. But before you do that, I ask you to remember that love will be the foundation of an abiding and deepening relationship. No other ties are more tender, no other vows more sacred than those you now assume. If you are able to keep the

vows you take here today, not because of any religious or civic law, but out of a desire to love and be loved by another person fully, without limitation, then your life will have joy and the home you establish will be a place in which you both will find the direction of your growth, your freedom, and your responsibility."

If the couple is reading their own written vows, then now is the time to ask them to read (traditionally, the groom goes first, and then the bride). If the couple is using generic vows, then you'll ask them to repeat after you. Make sure that you speak clearly, and only say one line at a time so it's easy for the couple to follow along.

Below are some examples of generic vows for you to consider. Remember that when you're performing a ceremony using generic vows, you need to say the vows one line at a time with the groom repeating, and then one at a time with the bride repeating.

Example A: *"Please repeat after me...*

I, [NAME], take you, [NAME],

to be my lawfully wedded [husband/wife],

to have and to hold,

from this day forward,

for better, for worse,

for richer, for poorer,

in sickness, and in health,

until death do us part [or "for as long as we both shall live"]."

Example B: *"Please repeat after me…*

I, [NAME], take you, [NAME],

to be my [husband/wife].

I promise to be true to you

in good times and in bad,

in sickness and in health.

I will love you and honor you

all the days of my life."

Example C: *"Please repeat after me…*

I, [NAME], take you, [NAME],

to be my [husband/wife],

my partner in life and my one true love.

I will cherish our union

and love you more each day

than I did the day before.

I will trust you and respect you,

laugh with you and cry with you,

loving you faithfully

through good times and bad,

regardless of the obstacles we may face together.

I give you my hand, my heart, and my love,

from this day forward,

for as long as we both shall live."

The Ceremony: Exchange of Rings

T he exchange of rings is when the couple gives each other wedding bands. This symbolizes the bond created by the marriage, as well as displaying their love for one another.

As the officiant, you will want to cue that it's time to exchange the rings. Consider this cue:

"These rings are symbols of eternity and the unbroken circle of love. Love freely given has no beginning and no end. Today you have chosen to exchange rings, as a sign of your love for each other, and as a seal of the promises you make this day."

Whoever is holding the rings should get them out and hand them to you, so you can give them to the couple when needed. You will be asking the couple to repeat after you. It is traditional for the groom to go first, then the bride. Longer prompts would require the couple to repeat one line at a time.

Below are some examples for you to consider:

Example A: *"Please look into [NAME'S] eyes, and place the ring, a symbol of your love for [her/him], on [her/ his] hand and say:*

With this ring, I thee wed."

Example B: *"Please look into [NAME'S] eyes, and place the ring on [her/ his] hand and say:*

I give you this ring, as a daily reminder of my love for you."

Example C: *"Please look into [NAME'S] eyes, and place the ring on [her/ his] hand and say:*

Just as this ring encircles your finger,

so does my love encircle your heart.

May this ring forever be a symbol

of my growing love for you.

With this ring, I thee wed."

The Ceremony: Unity Ceremony

A unity ceremony is another symbol for the bond of marriage and the joining of two families. Some couples may opt to include a unity ceremony, but in my experience, most do not unless they have a family tradition. There are many different types of unity ceremonies that can be performed, but the most common are the candle ceremony and the sand ceremony.

In a candle ceremony, two small candles are lit (traditionally by each of the mothers) and then placed on either side of a ceremonial table. The couple then takes these smaller candles and lights one large candle together. This symbolizes the joining of two families and the coming together of two individuals.

A sand ceremony is a bit more involved but can be very beautiful. Sand is poured from two separate vessels into a single vessel by both the bride and groom, and as they pour their sand into the vessel, they say a few words about their relationship. Once the sand is in the vessel, it can be preserved as a beautiful reminder of the wedding day.

Both of these ceremonies are very simple but can be very meaningful to couples and their families. If the couples are going to include a unity ceremony, they should choose one that feels most special to them, and consult any family members that will be involved.

The Ceremony: Words of Encouragement/Final Blessing

This is the last blessing before the presentation. You may also think of this as your closing remarks. It's your opportunity as the officiant to remind the couple of the commitment they just took, and to wish them success in their marriage. When giving words of encouragement, I prefer to speak directly to the couple.

The remainder of the ceremony is fairly cookie-cutter, so this is your last opportunity to speak freely and tie in your theme. Use this opportunity to end on a positive note. No one wants to hear about how the couple is going to Hell in a hand-basket. Keep your closing remarks light and positive, and wish them well for their future together.

The sample ceremony scripts give examples of how to weave in your theme during this section, and below are some generic examples that you can use:

Example A: "[GROOM] and [BRIDE], as the two of you have joined this marriage, uniting as husband and wife, and as you this day affirm your love for one another, I would ask that you always remember to cherish each other as special and unique individuals. And that you respect the thoughts, ideas, and suggestions of one another. Be able to forgive, do not hold grudges, and live each day so that you may share it together. As from this day forward, you shall be each other's home, comfort and refuge, your marriage strengthened by your love and respect."

Example B: *"[GROOM] and [BRIDE],*

May you have enough happiness to keep you sweet,

Enough trials to keep you strong,

Enough sorrow to keep you human,

Enough hope to keep you happy,

Enough failure to keep you humble,

Enough success to keep you eager,

Enough friends to give you comfort,

Enough wealth to meet your needs,

Enough enthusiasm to look forward,

Enough faith to banish despair,

Enough determination to make each day better than yesterday."

Example C, which is taken from "Blessing for a

Marriage" by James Dillet Freeman:

"*[GROOM] and [BRIDE]*,

May your marriage bring you all the exquisite excitements a marriage should bring,

and may life grant you also patience, tolerance, and understanding.

May you always need one another - not so much to fill your emptiness

as to help you to know your fullness.

A mountain needs a valley to be complete; the valley does not make the mountain less,

but more; and the valley is more a valley because it has a mountain towering over it.

So let it be with you and you.

May you need one another, but not out of weakness.

May you want one another, but not out of lack.

May you entice one another, but not compel one another.

May you embrace one another, but not out encircle one another.

May you succeed in all important ways with one another, and not fail in the little graces.

May you look for things to praise, often say, "I love you!" and take no notice of small faults.

If you have quarrels that push you apart,

may both of you hope to have good sense enough to take the first step back.

May you enter into the mystery which is the awareness of one another's presence,

no more physical than spiritual, warm and near when you are side by side,

and warm and near when you are in separate rooms or even distant cities.

May you have happiness, and may you find it making one another happy.

May you have love, and may you find it loving one another."

The Ceremony: Pronouncement of Marriage

The pronouncement is when the officiant declares the couple married. This is required in most states, so do not skip it! Below is the traditional pronouncement, but you don't need to use these exact words:

"By the power vested in me by [STATE or MINISTRY], I now pronounce you husband and wife."

The Ceremony: The Kiss

The kiss is when the couple kisses for their first time as a married couple, and usually follows immediately after the pronouncement. Your job is to simply cue the couple to kiss.

Pro Tip: Immediately after you cue the kiss, you should move out of the way FAST. This is a moment that the wedding photographer will want to capture. And no offense, but the couple won't want you in that picture. Consider coordinating with the photographer in advance, so you know which way to move. The couple will appreciate having a perfect, officiant-less wedding kiss picture.

Consider the following cues:

Example A*: "You may now kiss the bride!"*

Example B*: "You may now kiss each other!"*

The Ceremony: Presentation

The presentation is the ceremonial introduction to the married couple, and usually includes their names. Some couples may prefer "Mr. and Mrs.," while others want each of their names called individually, so be sure to ask the couple their preference.

Speak loudly and project, because some attendees may already be clapping after the pronouncement and kiss. After you complete the presentation, you should encourage everyone to stand and clap.

Some examples of the presentation include:

Example A – Mr. and Mrs.*: "I present to you, for the first time ever, Mr. and Mrs. [GROOM LAST NAME]."*

Example B – First Names*: "I present to you, for the first time ever, the newly married couple, [GROOM] and [BRIDE]."*

The Ceremony: Recessional

The recessional is when the wedding party walks back down the aisle and exits the venue, usually to music. The recessional occurs in the reverse order of the processional, with the couple exiting together first.

As the officiant, you should stay at the altar until the couple exits the venue. Then you may exit with the wedding attendees. Consider coordinating with the photographer to see if there's a place they'd like you to stand during the recessional.

Get Prepared: How to Prepare for the Ceremony

Although you've written the ceremony script, it's not going to be as easy as reading off a printed page. Now that the ceremony is constructed, you need to prepare properly for the big day.

Step 1: Transcribe Your Script into an Appropriate Notebook

Even if you plan to memorize the ceremony (which is definitely not required), I strongly recommend that you transcribe your script into an appropriate notebook. Remember: you will be standing in front of everyone and will be in several photos. Loose-leaf papers and legal pads are not acceptable for this occasion.

You could use an eReader or iPad with a simple case, but both options come with drawbacks. I've found that there is nothing more frustrating than having to worry about an electronic device's battery dying during the ceremony, and you should also consider how the eReader will fit inside your pocket or leave room for your hands to properly gesture.

When you're selecting a notebook for your ceremony script, you should consider three important factors:

1. **Size**: You want something that will fit in one hand while it's open. Don't assume that you will have a podium on which you can place a large binder or notepad. The smaller size also leaves your other hand free to hold a microphone (if needed), gesture, flip pages, and receive/ hand out the wedding bands. I personally use half letter size (5.5" x 8.5") or smaller.

2. **Appearance**: I recommend something black and leather (or faux-leather) bound. Don't buy anything too colorful or flashy; you do not want your notebook to draw any attention. If you want to snazzy it up, then consider getting a notebook with gold binding.

3. **Price**: What is your budget? It's not necessary to break the bank on this purchase (but you certainly can if you'd like to). There are plenty of affordable, nice-looking notebooks that will suit your needs.

When I first began officiating weddings, I would hand-write the script in my notebook. Over time, I've found that I prefer printing and taping or stapling it to the pages. Do whatever works best for you. Either way, be careful that the script is secure and won't blow away in a sudden gesture or gust of wind.

Regardless of your approach, I recommend that you (a) write in large, easy-to-read font, (b) include large, bold headings indicating the current section, (c) format sentences and paragraphs in a way that gives clues on when to pause, and (d) write the next section on the bottom of each page. This will help you not lose track of or find your place as you glance down, especially if you go off-script, and will help ensure a smooth transition between sections.

If you want recommendations on appropriate notebooks for the occasion, please visit instantofficiant.com/resources.

Step 2: Practice, Practice, Practice

One of the most important things to do as a wedding officiant is to be familiar with the ceremony. Read it through several times, and make sure you know all the parts.

Knowing the words and order is only half of the equation, though. You also need to make sure that your presentation is spot-on. Make sure to practice and pay attention to these four things:

1. **Volume**: Will you be using a microphone? How loudly will your voice carry in the space where the ceremony is taking place? Be prepared for either scenario.
2. **Pacing**: Most speakers tend to speed up when

nervous. Don't rush through it at top speed. Make sure to pay attention to each word and phrase so that each one has an impact.

3. **Inflection**: You want your voice to sound excited and happy, not strained or nervous.
4. **Eye-Contact**: Even if you are working off a script, you need to make eye contact with people to help connect with them.

You may want to videotape yourself practicing so that you can get an idea of how it sounds and looks (you'll especially want to do this if the couple plans to videotape the ceremony). Practicing in front of a friend is also recommended.

Step 3: Confirm Important Points with the Couple

In the weeks leading up to the wedding, you will want to touch base with the couple to confirm three important items:

1. **Dates, Location, and Time Commitment**: Be sure you know exactly where you need to be, and when.
2. **Your Attire**: Run your wardrobe by the couple to make sure it is acceptable. Sometimes the couple may ask for minor adjustments. For example, I've attended weddings where the couple wanted the groom to be the only person wearing a bowtie.

3. **The Wedding License**: Make sure that the couple has applied for and received their wedding license because you'll need to sign it after the ceremony.

Once you've handled all of this, you're ready for the big day.

The Big Day: Checklist

A llow plenty of time to get ready and to arrive at the ceremony location early (at least 45 minutes before the scheduled start time). Before you walk out the door, follow this seven-item checklist to make sure you have everything you need:

1. **Your Script**: This one is important. I've made the mistake of leaving it in my hotel room before, and it's stressful (and easily avoidable). Thankfully, I realized it with plenty of time to go back to retrieve it.

2. **Other Documents**: This one is a little more important than it might seem. Make sure you have your government-issued ID, as well as your ordination papers (if needed in your state) and the certificate of marriage (if the couple gave it to you for safekeeping).

3. **A Pen**: You will need a pen to sign the marriage certificate. Don't rely on someone else to supply one; bring your own. Some

marriage certificates specify a certain color ink, so either confirm what you need ahead of time or bring both a black and blue pen.

4. **Your Outfit**: Are you sure you have everything? Pants, shirt, jacket, tie, cufflinks, tie-clip, shoes, appropriate socks, dress, tights, top hat, etc.? Don't risk it; double-check.

5. **Hair, Makeup, and Grooming**: You want to look your best in any photos or video taken of you at the wedding, so make sure to take care with hair, makeup, and grooming. This includes ensuring that your hair is styled properly, and makeup is applied tastefully as needed.

6. **A Gift**: If it's a friend's wedding, then you're probably going to bring a gift. If it's not a friend's wedding, and the couple is paying you to officiate, then you're not expected to bring a gift.

7. **Anything Else the Couple Requested**: Maybe you're bringing your own sound system? Or perhaps you agreed to pick up the coffee on the way? Whatever it is, make sure you have it.

The Big Day: Lead-Up to the Ceremony

Once you arrive at the venue (again, at least 45 minutes before the scheduled start time), you still have plenty of work to do to make sure the ceremony goes off without a hitch.

Task 1: Check-in with the Couple

First and foremost, it's important to check in with the couple. Make sure they're both feeling good and haven't gotten too nervous. If either of them looks like they need a minute to calm down, take them aside and give them a quick pep talk.

Task 2: Orient Yourself

Next, take a few minutes to do a final walk-through of the space and make sure you know where everything is. This will help you avoid any last-minute surprises or embarrassments.

Task 3: Say Hello

Introduce yourself to any wedding party participants that you haven't met yet, especially those that you will need to cue during the ceremony. This may include:

- Best Man/ Maid of Honor
- Groomsmen/ Bridesmaids
- Parents
- Ring Bearers/ Flower Girls (and their parents)
- Readers
- Wedding Planners
- Photographers/ Videographers
- DJ

Don't spend too much time chatting, though, because there is still plenty to do.

Task 4: Remind People About their Cues

It's helpful to provide a reminder to anyone that you are going to cue during the ceremony, and the words that they're expected to say (if it's not a "repeat after me" scenario). This could include the father-of-the-bride (for the "Giving of the Bride"), readers (for the "Readings"), photographer (for photo cues), DJ (for musical cues), or any other cues that you have arranged with the couple.

Task 5: Resist Any Temptations

Sometimes wedding parties drink before the ceremony, to loosen the nerves or to celebrate. Resist the urge to join in, and stay sober for the ceremony. An officiant that is under the influence will not set the tone that you want for the wedding, and could potentially ruin the day for everyone involved. You can wait until after the ceremony to treat yourself to a beverage.

Task 6: Check Audio Setup

Make sure the audio is working properly, and that you know how to operate the microphone. This is especially important if you are using a corded microphone. Test the mic before the ceremony starts, to avoid any embarrassing mishaps.

Task 7: Confirm You Have Everything Needed for the Ceremony

Make sure everything you need to conduct the ceremony. If the best man is holding the rings, confirm that they have them in their pocket. If a Bible or other religious text will be used for any portion of the ceremony, make sure you have it with you. And of course, make sure that you have your script in hand.

Task 8: Expect the Unexpected

OK, so this is technically more of a mindset than a task.

Just because you've finalized the script, don't expect that there won't be additional changes. Keep in mind that you want to make the couple happy, and be prepared for any curveballs they may throw at you (including last-minute changes). This is another place where that pen you brought comes in handy!

Task 9: Try to Relax

The best way to make sure the wedding ceremony goes off without a hitch is to stay calm and relaxed. The couple chose you as their officiant because they trust your judgment, so use it and everything will be fine. If you're properly prepared and go in with confidence, there's no reason why you can't deliver a fantastic wedding ceremony.

The Big Day: The Wedding Ceremony Itself

Everyone is lined up, and you're ready to get started. You're prepared for this moment, so don't be nervous. Try to remember these seven points during your execution.

(1) Speak Clearly and with Confidence

Be yourself, be genuine, and let your personality show. Speak clearly and with confidence; you know this ceremony inside and out. The wedding ceremony should feel like a conversation between you and the couple, not a formal speech. You don't want your delivery to detract from the ceremony itself.

(2) Watch Your Volume

Make sure that your voice is carrying, so people in the back can hear you, but try not to shout. You don't want people getting cranky because they can't hear what's going on.

(3) Be Mindful of Your Timing and Pacing

It's all too easy to rush. During the actual ceremony, time will tick by faster than you ever imagined. But don't be tempted to speed things up. Slow down, take a deep breath... relax! All that rushing won't help anything.

(4) Remember to Vary the Inflection of Your Voice

This is an important one. You don't want to sound like a robot during the ceremony. Be sure to use different inflections for different parts of the ceremony. You practiced this already, so you've got it!

(5) Make Eye Contact

You're not there to read a speech. You're there to connect with the people you're speaking to, so make good use of your eyes! Look at the couple as they turn toward you, everyone in the front row, and even those sitting in the back. It'll help the crowd feel more engaged in the ceremony.

(6) Get Out of the Pictures

Remember to move out of the way when needed so the photographer can capture great pictures for the couple. You should have already coordinated this with the photographer. At a minimum, move out of the frame during the first kiss.

(7) Have Fun!

This is your time to shine, so enjoy it! This is one of

the happiest days of the couple's life, and you're a part of that. Let yourself get caught up in the moment, and have some fun with it!

The Big Day: After the Wedding

A wedding officiant's job is not done just because the ceremony is over. There are some final steps you need to take care of to make everything official.

Step 1: Sign the Marriage License

Before everyone starts partying at the reception, you need to pull people aside to sign the marriage license.

Fill out the marriage license completely, and get all of the necessary signatures. For most marriage licenses, you will need signatures from the couple, two witnesses, and the officiant.

Make sure to read the license in detail before signing, because sometimes they have seemingly odd requirements. For example, some jurisdictions require you to use certain color ink when signing.

Note that some wedding resources suggest stopping the wedding to sign the marriage license. Personally, I think this is crazy. It completely ruins the momentum of the ceremony. You can do it after the ceremony and before the reception.

Step 2: Return the Marriage License

Return the license to the appropriate office within the required time. It's usually the officiant's job to return the marriage license, but the couple may decide to entrust a close friend or family member instead. Just make sure it's covered!

I recommend making a copy or taking a picture of the marriage license before returning it, so you have a backup in case anything goes wrong (like getting lost in the mail).

Most jurisdictions allow you to mail the license, but others may require you to drop it off at the appropriate county building near where you performed the ceremony. Just make sure that you address it appropriately, and follow any other return instructions.

The license will specify the required timing to return the license. It is usually within a few days of the wedding. If this is not done within the required timeframe, there may be penalties involved or issues with getting the license certified. Therefore, I prefer to handle it on the day of the ceremony whenever possible.

Step 3: Don't Overstay Your Welcome

You should have already discussed the couple's expectations regarding which events you will attend. If you have not received an invite to the reception, you should assume you are not invited. Resist the urge to stop by the reception to say hello, unless you are certain the couple wants you there.

If you do choose to stick around, make sure to pace yourself and don't overdo it on the alcohol. You want to stay sharp and ready for any questions that might come up regarding the ceremony you performed, or other general officiant issues.

Step 4: Consider Sending the Script as a Gift

When you get home, consider sending a nicely formatted copy of the wedding ceremony script to the happy couple. Wedding days are very emotional and charged with nervous energy and excitement. It is highly likely that the couple only really heard a quarter to half of the ceremony. Even a digital copy of the script would be greatly appreciated, as it can provide a keepsake for the couple to reflect on their big day.

Concluding Remarks

After reading this book, you have all of the tools you need to create the perfect wedding ceremony. You know how to become an officiant, when and how to engage with the couple to create a meaningful ceremony, the various parts of a wedding ceremony (including sample wording), how to write and prepare for the ceremony, how to conduct the ceremony, and what to do afterwards. Even if you are preparing for your first wedding ceremony, you should have it well under control.

In the remainder of this book I have included two full sample wedding ceremony scripts, so you can see how a full ceremony comes together. Please feel free to leverage these when creating your own ceremony variations.

I have also included some special thanks to people who inspired me and provided guidance along the way. After all, you can't discuss weddings without adding at least a little sappiness.

As you move forward, please remember that

weddings are one of the most important days in a couple's life, and the officiant plays a vital role in the ceremony. When it comes to planning for this day, there is much to consider and take into account. You should not take your job lightly. But it is a manageable task and a rewarding experience. If you're lucky enough to be asked to officiate a wedding, don't shy away from the responsibility. Best of luck!

Sample Ceremony Script 1: Generic, Theme of Love

Below is a sample script using the theme of "love" and a serious tone. It uses generic wedding vows. If you need something off-the-shelf, then this is a good place to start. If you want an example of something more personalized, then read our other script sample.

1. Prelude/ Seating of the Guests

[I would stand in front while everyone takes their seats.]

2. Processional

[The wedding party walks down the aisle. I start talking when the BRIDE and FATHER-OF-THE-BRIDE arrive at the altar.]

3. Giving of the Bride

Who supports [BRIDE] in her marriage to [GROOM]?

[FATHER-OF-THE-BRIDE]: "I do."

[GROOM and FATHER-OF-THE-BRIDE would shake hands.]

[I would gesture for the FATHER-OF-THE-BRIDE to sit, and for the GROOM to come stand next to BRIDE.]

4. Words of Welcome/ Introduction

Welcome friends, relatives, and distinguished guests. We're glad you could join us in celebrating love. Our large and ever-changing planet is controlled by love. It is that which makes our human existence meaningful and beautiful. The greatest gift bestowed on humanity is the gift of love freely given between two people.

Please be seated.

5. Special Dedication/ Remembrances

It is my honor to celebrate the family members of [BRIDE] and [GROOM]. Your love, dedication, and fidelity has profoundly shaped their lives. Thank you for showing them the possibilities inherent when loving another.

I would also like to thank those of you that have traveled far to be here today. We are all glad that you could make it.

6. Address to Congregation/ Opening Remarks

Love is the reason we are here. In marriage, we not only say, "I love you today", but also, "I promise to love you for all of our tomorrows."

[GROOM] and [BRIDE], in the days ahead of you, there will be stormy times and good times, times of conflict and times of joy. I ask you to remember this advice:

Never go to bed angry.

Let your love be stronger than your anger.

Learn the wisdom of compromise, for it is better to bend than to break.

Believe the best of your beloved rather than the worst.

Confide in your partner and ask for help when you need it.

Remember that true friendship is the basis for any lasting relationship.

Give your spouse the same courtesies and kindnesses you bestow on your friends.

Say "I love you" every day.

7. Readings

I'd like to welcome [NAME] up for the first reading.

[The READER would complete the selected reading, then take his/her seat.]

...

I'd like to welcome [NAME] up for the second reading.

[The READER would complete the selected reading, then take his/her seat.]

...

8. Support of Community

Two people in love do not live in isolation. Their love is a source of strength with which they may nourish not only each other but also the world around them. And in turn, we, their community of friends and family, have a responsibility to this couple. By our steadfast care, respect, and love, we can support their marriage and the new family they are creating today.

Will everyone please rise?

I have an important question for all of you, the appropriate response to which is "we will."

Will you who are present here today, surround [GROOM] and [BRIDE] in love, offering them the joys of your friendship, and supporting them in their marriage?

[ALL]: "We will."

Thank you, and please be seated.

9. Declaration of Intent/ Charge

Entering into marriage is a decision that requires careful thought and consideration.

[GROOM], do you understand and accept the responsibilities of marriage, and do you promise to always love, honor, and cherish [BRIDE]?

[GROOM]: "I do."

[BRIDE], do you understand and accept the responsibilities of marriage, and do you promise to always love, honor, and cherish [GROOM]?

[BRIDE]: "I do."

10. Exchange of Vows

We've come to the point of your ceremony where you're going to say your vows to one another. But before you do that, I ask you to remember that love will be the foundation of an abiding and deepening relationship. No other ties are more tender, no other vows more sacred than those you now assume. If you are able to keep the vows you take here today, not because of any religious or civic law, but out of a desire to love and be loved by another person fully, without limitation, then your life will have joy and the home you establish will be a place in which you both will find the direction of your growth, your freedom, and your responsibility.

[GROOM], please repeat after me.

[The GROOM repeats after each line.]

I, [GROOM], take you, [BRIDE],

to be my lawfully wedded wife,

to have and to hold,

from this day forward,

for better, for worse,

for richer, for poorer,

in sickness, and in health,

until death do us part.

[BRIDE], please repeat after me.

[The BRIDE repeats after each line.]

I, [BRIDE], take you, [GROOM],

to be my lawfully wedded husband,

to have and to hold,

from this day forward,

for better, for worse,

for richer, for poorer,

in sickness, and in health,

until death do us part.

11. Exchange of Rings

May I please have the rings?

[I would accept the rings from whomever was holding them, and hold them up for the guests to see.]

These rings are symbols of eternity and the unbroken

circle of love. Love freely given has no beginning and no end. Today you have chosen to exchange rings, as a sign of your love for each other, and as a seal of the promises you make this day.

[GROOM], please look into her eyes, and place the ring, a symbol of your love for [BRIDE], on her hand and say:

I give you this ring, as a daily reminder of my love for you.

[The GROOM places the ring on the BRIDE'S finger and repeats.]

[BRIDE], please look into his eyes, and place the ring, a symbol of your love for [GROOM], on his hand and say:

I give you this ring, as a daily reminder of my love for you.

[The BRIDE places the ring on the GROOM'S finger and repeats.]

12. Words of Encouragement/ Final Blessing

[GROOM] and [BRIDE], as the two of you have joined this marriage, uniting as husband and wife, and as you this day affirm your love for one another, I would ask that you always remember to cherish each other as special and unique individuals. And that you respect the thoughts, ideas, and suggestions of one another. Be able to forgive, do not hold grudges, and live each day so that you may share it together. As from this day forward, you shall be each other's home, comfort and refuge, your marriage strengthened by your love and respect.

13. Pronouncement of Marriage

And now, by the power vested in me by [STATE or MINISTRY], I now pronounce you husband and wife.

14. The Kiss

You may now kiss the bride!

[I would move quickly out of the way for the photographer, and BRIDE and GROOM would kiss.]

15. Presentation

I present to you, for the first time ever, Mr. and Mrs. [GROOM LAST NAME].

16. Recessional

[Finally, the wedding party walks down the aisle in reverse order, and the ceremony ends. I would make sure that the marriage certificate gets signed after the couple is done with their receiving line, but before the reception.]

Sample Ceremony Script 2: Personalized, Theme of Growth

Below is a sample script using the theme of "growth" and a joyful, playful tone. The couple prepared their own wedding vows. The address to the congregation uses personal anecdotes to show you how they can be woven into the ceremony, and would obviously need to be changed if you used this script as a starting point.

1. Prelude/ Seating of the Guests

[I would stand in front while everyone takes their seats]

2. Processional

[The wedding party walks down the aisle. I start talking when the BRIDE arrives at the altar, and the FATHER-OF-THE-BRIDE takes his seat (because there is no "Giving of the Bride").]

3. Words of Welcome/ Introduction

Welcome friends and family!

Today marks the day that [GROOM] and [BRIDE] make their union official.

Each and every one of you has been a special part of their lives, and they are thrilled to have you gathered here in celebration with them.

Today is a good day, and we're excited to share it together.

Please be seated.

4. Special Dedication/ Remembrances

I would like to take a moment to recognize two very special guests that are joining us virtually: [NAMES].

We wish you could be here in person, but we are so happy that you can witness the wedding on the livestream.

If you experience any technical difficulties, please direct your strongly worded letters to [GROOM]'s brother and best man, [NAME].

5. Address to Congregation/ Opening Remarks

For those of you that don't know me, my name is [NAME]. I've known [GROOM] since middle school, which is forever ago. And I've known [BRIDE] since shortly after they started dating… which is also basically forever ago.

As a side note, my wife and I dated for 7 years before getting married, so I'm not judging.

In preparation for the ceremony, I asked [GROOM] and [BRIDE] to recount some stories about their early time together. Surprisingly, I had not heard them before. And thankfully, they were appropriate to share here today.

[BRIDE]'s story was about how she needed to badger [GROOM] for a second date. Not because [GROOM] didn't want to go on one - he had a lovely time on the first date. [GROOM] was just slow to respond, because he can get easily distracted.

[GROOM]'s story was about an early date, it may have even been their second date, when [GROOM] tried to wander around a museum with a ceramic coffee mug because there was no sign saying he couldn't. [BRIDE] was mortified and thought it was obviously not permitted. [GROOM] didn't care, and figured "what's the worst that could happen?" Security eventually made [GROOM] return to the café, but not before they took in a few nice sips and exhibits.

I like both of those stories because they tell the same tale. [BRIDE] is pragmatic, and [GROOM] is a dreamer. And it's those differences that make them work well together.

In marriage, two people turn to each other in search of a greater fulfillment than either can achieve alone. [GROOM] and [BRIDE] both already know that they can achieve more together. [BRIDE] encourages [GROOM] to be more attentive and productive, and [GROOM] encourages [BRIDE] to be more daring and carefree.

But just because it works well doesn't mean it's always easy. You have learned over the years what it means to love one another. Through good times and bad times, I have had the honor and privilege to witness how both of you have learned how to grow and thrive as a couple.

Today's wedding isn't the end of that growth; it's just the beginning. Marriage is about continuing to learn how to live your lives together as one couple, not as two separate lives. It means continually moving forward as a unit, and working together towards the shared success of your family.

I'm proud to call you my friends, and I look forward to seeing what more you will achieve together. Let nothing stand in the way of your marriage.

6. Readings

I'd like to welcome [BRIDE]'s sister [NAME] up for the first reading.

[The READER would complete the selected reading, then take his/her seat.]

…

I'd like to welcome [GROOM]'s sister [NAME] up for the second reading.

[The READER would complete the selected reading, then take his/her seat.]

…

7. Declaration of Intent/ Charge

It's already time to say "I do." So, [GROOM] and [BRIDE]… are you ready to do this?!

[BRIDE and GROOM]: "Yes!"

Friends and family, are you all ready to witness this?!

[ALL]: "Yes!"

LET'S DO THIS!

[GROOM], do you promise to keep [BRIDE] as your favorite person -

to laugh with her, go on adventures with her,

support her through life's tough moments,

be proud of her, grow old with her, and find new reasons to love her every day?

[GROOM]: "I do."

[BRIDE], do you promise to keep [GROOM] as your favorite person -

to laugh with him, go on adventures with him,

support him through life's tough moments,

be proud of him, grow old with him, and find new reasons to love him every day?

[BRIDE]: "I do."

8. Exchange of Vows

The couple will now exchange the vows they've prepared for each other.

[GROOM], please go ahead and read your vows to [BRIDE].

[The GROOM would now read the vows he prepared.]

…

[BRIDE], please go ahead and read your vows to [GROOM].

[The BRIDE would now read the vows she prepared.]

…

9. Exchange of Rings

May I please have the rings?

[I would accept the rings from whomever was holding them, and hold them up for the guests to see.]

Today you have chosen to exchange rings, as a reminder of your love and a seal of the promises you make this day.

[GROOM], place the ring on [BRIDE]'s hand, look her in the eyes, and repeat after me:

"With this ring,

I promise to stand with you as we share this life,

and cherish the memories we make together."

[The GROOM places the ring on the BRIDE'S finger and repeats.]

[BRIDE], place the ring on [GROOM]'s hand, look him in the eyes, and repeat after me:

"With this ring,

I promise to stand with you as we share this life,

and cherish the memories we make together."

[The BRIDE places the ring on the GROOM'S finger and repeats.]

10. Words of Encouragement/ Final Blessing

Today we've said some magic words to make things official in the state's eyes. But the power of your wedding vows is merely a reflection of a reality that already exists in your hearts and minds.

Nothing we say today will ensure a long and happy, satisfying, and committed marriage. Only your love for one another, and your integrity to make your commitment real, can do that.

I would ask that you always remember to cherish each other as special and unique individuals. And that you respect the thoughts, ideas, and suggestions of one another. Be able to forgive, do not hold grudges, and live each day so that you may share it together. I have confidence in you, and I wish you both a lifetime of success and happiness.

11. Pronouncement of Marriage

And now, by the power vested in me by [STATE or MINISTRY], I now pronounce you husband and wife.

12. The Kiss

You may now kiss the bride!

[I would move quickly out of the way for the photographer, and BRIDE and GROOM would kiss.]

13. Presentation

I present to you, for the first time ever, the newly married couple, [GROOM] and [BRIDE].

14. Recessional

[Finally, the wedding party walks down the aisle in reverse order, and the ceremony ends. I would make sure that the marriage certificate gets signed after the couple is done with their receiving line, but before the reception.]

Special Thanks

———————————— ❦ ————————————

I would like to take a moment to give special thanks to people who provided me guidance, inspiration, and assistance along the way.

Thank you to the countless officiants who have documented their experiences, recommendations, and ceremonies online. Reading through your materials helped me understand what is required of a wedding officiant, as well as common phrasing for various parts of the ceremony (many of which appear as samples in this book). I hope that this book similarly serves as a source of inspiration for someone else.

Thank you to all of the couples who entrusted me with the responsibility of serving as their officiant. It was always a wonderful and unique experience, and I am honored to have been involved.

Thank you to my friends Tom and Jon for your help with organizing and editing this book. It may have never been completed without you.

Thank you to my beautiful wife Nikki for believing in me, particularly when I didn't believe in myself.

And finally, thank you to <u>you, the reader,</u> for purchasing this book! If you have any suggestions or recommendations for me to consider for the next edition, then please reach out to me at contact@instantofficiant.com. I would love to hear from you!

Made in United States
Troutdale, OR
04/03/2024

18910502R00060